D1172061

Scientists at Work

Marine Biologists

Julie Haydon

Smart Apple Media

Smart Apple Media
1980 Lookout Drive
North Mankato
Minnesota 56003

Library of Congress Cataloging-in-Publication Data

Haydon, Julie.
  Marine biologists / by Julie Haydon.
    p. cm. — (Scientists at work)
  ISBN 1-58340-540-2 (alk. paper)
  1. Marine biology—Vocational guidance—Juvenile literature. 2. Marine biologists—Juvenile literature.
  [1. Marine biologists. 2. Marine biology—Vocational guidance. 3. Vocational guidance.] I. Title.
  II. Scientists at work (Smart Apple Media)

  QH91.45.H38 2004
  578.77'023—dc22   2003070417

First Edition
9 8 7 6 5 4 3 2 1

First published in 2004 by
MACMILLAN EDUCATION AUSTRALIA PTY LTD
627 Chapel Street, South Yarra, Australia, 3141

Associated companies and representatives throughout the world.

Copyright © Julie Haydon 2004

Edited by Sally Woollett
Text and cover design by The Modern Art Production Group
Page layout by Raul Diche
Photo research by Jesmondene Senbergs
Printed in China

Acknowledgements
The author and the publisher are grateful to the following for permission to reproduce copyright material:

Cover photograph: Marine biologist lecturing students, courtesy of Great Southern Stock.

AAP, p. 25; Associated Press EFE, p. 9; Jean-Paul Ferrero/Auscape, p. 27; David B. Fleetham–OSF/Auscape, p. 24; Ken Smith Laboratory, Scripps Institute of Oceanography–OSF/Auscape, p. 10; D. Parer & E. Parer-Cook/Auscape, p. 21; Claude Steelman/Survival Anglia–Oxford/Auscape, p. 28; Australian War Memorial, p. 7; Corbis, pp. 5, 19; CSIRO Marine Research, pp. 14 (top left), 15 (middle left); Curtin University, p. 15 (bottom left); Great Barrier Reef Marine Park Authority, pp. 15 (top right), 21; Great Southern Stock, p. 12; Image Library, pp. 14 (right), 29; Clay Bryce/Lochman Transparencies, p. 15 (top left); Jiri Lochman/Lochman Transparencies, p. 4; Kelvin Aitken/Marine Themes, p. 8; Melbourne Aquarium, pp. 13, 30; Marah Newman, p. 22; NOAA Photo Library, pp. 6, 14 (bottom left), 18, 26; Photodisc, p. 15 (middle right, bottom right); Photolibrary.com/SPL, p. 23; British Antarctic Survey/Science Photo Library, p. 20; TOPP, p. 17; TRCC, p. 16.

Author acknowledgements
Many thanks to Marah Newman, for kindly agreeing to be interviewed for this book, and to Dr. Gina Newton for her review of the first draft. Thanks also to Dr. Randall Kochevar for his help with the TOPP case study and to Dr. Steve O'Shea, Dr. Cindy Lee Van Dover, Dr. Mark Norman, John Forsythe, Dr. Roland Anderson, Narelle Hall, Jane Miller, Dr. Joseph Wible, Nick Falcone, Cindy Clark, and Dora Dalton. A special thanks to Gil Hewlett of the Vancouver Aquarium for telling me the true octopus escape story.

While every care has been taken to trace and acknowledge copyright, the publisher tenders their apologies for any accidental infringement where copyright has proved untraceable. Where the attempt has been unsuccessful, the publisher welcomes information that would redress the situation.

Please note
At the time of printing, the Internet addresses appearing in this book were correct. Owing to the dynamic nature of the Internet, however, we cannot guarantee that all these addresses will remain correct.

Contents

Glossary words

When you see a word printed in **bold**, you can look up its meaning in the glossary on page 31.

What is a marine biologist?

A marine biologist is a scientist who studies marine organisms. Marine organisms are animals, plants, and other living things that live in the oceans. Marine biologists study the bodies, behavior, and history of marine organisms. They also study how marine organisms interact with each other and their environments.

There are many different types of marine organisms, and a marine biologist cannot study them all. Most marine biologists specialize, which means they focus their studies in one area. For example, a marine biologist might study corals, crabs, fish, **microscopic** marine organisms, sea stars, seaweeds, squids, or whales.

A marine biologist's job is varied. It can involve working on a specially equipped research ship, diving to study marine life, and collecting marine samples. It can also involve performing experiments in a laboratory, analyzing data on a computer, writing up reports, and educating people about marine research and **conservation**.

Scientists
working together

Marine biologists often work with other marine scientists, such as physical oceanographers and marine geoscientists. Physical oceanographers study the physical processes and characteristics of oceans, such as waves, **currents**, tides, water temperature, and **salinity**. Marine geoscientists study the seabed and how it formed.

This marine biologist is studying a turtle.

The role of marine biologists

Marine biologists play an important role in our world. The oceans cover 71 percent of our planet and contain a huge variety of marine organisms. Marine biologists help us learn about these organisms and the **ecosystems** they live in.

Most of us may never see a real whale or a deep-sea fish, but thanks to marine biologists we can read about them, and look at pictures of them. The more marine biologists learn about marine life, the more we learn about life on Earth, and the connections between life forms.

Marine biologists also help us to plan ways of protecting marine organisms and their environments. These plans often involve managing what we take from and put in the oceans. This is important because the oceans are beautiful and full of life. They also provide us with many things, including:

- fish, **crustaceans**, turtles, and other organisms, used for food
- pearls, shells, and corals, used to make jewelry and ornaments
- skins of marine animals such as saltwater crocodiles, used for leather
- seaweed, which contains chemicals used in some toiletries, paints, and plastics
- oxygen, some of which is made by marine plants and plant-like organisms during a process called **photosynthesis**. Oxygen is in the air we must breathe to survive.
- areas for relaxation and for leisure activities

Marine biologists help monitor human activities that affect marine life. These activities include polluting waterways, introducing new types of marine life, and changing coastal environments. Governments use the information that marine biologists collect to help them develop marine management and conservation policies and laws.

Marine biologists also help to develop marine-based industries, such as **fisheries** and tourism.

The oceans provide us with many things, including food.

Marine biology in the past

Long ago, people learned that the sea was full of good things to eat. At first, people walked along the shore and waded into the shallows to catch and collect marine organisms. Later, people learned to make simple fishing tools, such as fish hooks, harpoons, and nets. They built rafts and boats to travel from place to place and to fish out at sea.

Tall tales about the sea

As fishermen, sailors, and explorers began to spend more time at sea, they told tales of mermaids and sea monsters. These made-up stories may have been based on sightings of large marine animals.

Recording marine life

A Greek scientist named Aristotle (384–322 BC) was one of the first marine biologists. In his book *History of Animals*, he described many marine organisms, including fish and **mollusks**. Aristotle did not have the equipment or knowledge to study deep-sea marine life, so he studied marine organisms that could be caught easily.

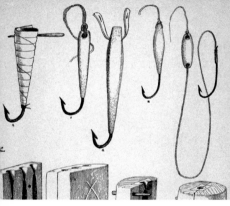

Long ago, people used simple fishing tools to catch marine organisms.

Key events in marine biology	350 B.C. Aristotle writes *History of Animals*.	1831 Charles Darwin begins work as a naturalist aboard the HMS *Beagle*. He collects marine samples, using a net to catch plankton.	1847 Joseph Hooker identifies some planktons as plant-like.
B.C. Prehistoric humans learn to catch and eat marine organisms.	1768 Captain James Cook begins the first of three voyages to explore all the oceans.	1830s Edward Forbes begins dredging the sea floor and discovers new organisms.	

Progress in marine biology

Over time, ships, charts, and **navigation** equipment improved, and long voyages became more common. These improvements made it easier to observe marine life and collect samples.

Voyages of exploration

In 1768, Captain James Cook, an English navigator, began the first of three voyages to explore the oceans. During the voyages, marine samples were collected. Charles Darwin, an English **naturalist**, worked aboard the HMS *Beagle* from 1831 to 1836. Darwin collected and studied many marine organisms.

Better ships and equipment

During the 1800s, other scientists began to focus their attention on life near the sea floor and on microscopic marine life. But it was in 1872 that marine biology took a giant leap forward when the *Challenger* expedition set out from Portsmouth, England.

HMS *Challenger*

The scientists and crew spent three-and-a-half years aboard the *Challenger* collecting samples and information about the oceans. They kept careful scientific records. The expedition was a huge success.

In the 1900s, more complex equipment was developed, such as scuba-diving gear, underwater cameras, and **submersibles**. Marine biologists could observe and record marine life in its natural **habitat** for a longer time.

Today, marine biologists use well-equipped marine research vessels, remotely operated vehicles, computers, **sonar**, satellites, powerful microscopes, and other tools to aid them in their work.

1872
HMS *Challenger* sets out on a three-and-a-half year scientific expedition of the oceans. Many new marine species are found.

1934
William Beebe and Otis Barton dive in the bathysphere to observe the deep sea.

1977
Hydrothermal sea vents are discovered. New marine species are found living around the vents.

1872
First permanent marine laboratory opens in Naples, Italy.

1943
Jacques Cousteau and Emile Gagnan develop the aqualung.

2001
Live giant squid babies are caught for the first time.

Important discoveries

Many important discoveries have helped marine biologists and other scientists learn more about marine life.

Life on the sea floor

During the 1830s and 1840s, Edward Forbes, a British naturalist, went on several expeditions to study the oceans. He was particularly interested in life on or near the sea floor. Using a tool known as a dredge, Forbes scooped up samples from the sea floor. He discovered many new organisms and recognized that marine life is different at different ocean depths.

Photosynthesis in water organisms

In 1847, English botanist Joseph Hooker recognized that tiny drifting **algae** called diatoms play the same role in water as green plants do on land. Algae and green plants provide animals with food and oxygen. Diatoms, like green plants, use the sun's energy to make their own food in a process called photosynthesis.

Fact Box

Diatoms and other organisms that drift together in water were given the collective name "plankton" by German scientist Victor Hensen in 1887. Plankton can be marine or freshwater organisms. Most plankton are tiny. Most food chains in water begin with plankton.

Most plankton are so small that they can only be seen through a microscope.

Life among hydrothermal vents

In 1977, a group of marine scientists aboard a submersible found deep-sea hot springs, called hydrothermal vents, on the floor of the Pacific Ocean. The scientists, led by Americans Dr. John Corliss and Dr. Robert Ballard, also found a rich assortment of marine organisms living among the vents. Many of the organisms had never been seen before. They included huge worms, clams, mussels, crabs, shrimps, and fish.

Sunlight is not able to reach the deep-sea floor. Scientists had previously believed that all food chains began with plants and plant-like organisms that made their own food using the sun's energy. Marine biologists discovered that **bacteria** at the hydrothermal vents use the energy of a chemical called hydrogen sulfide to make their own food. This process is called chemosynthesis. The bacteria are the base of the food chains at the vents.

This giant squid was caught off the northern coast of Spain in 2002.

Live giant squid

The giant squid is an **invertebrate** that lives in the deep sea and grows up to 43 feet (13 m) long. The bodies of adult giant squids sometimes wash up on beaches or are caught in fishing nets, but no adult giant squid has ever been seen alive. In 2001, a group of marine biologists, led by Dr. Steve O'Shea from New Zealand, set out on a voyage to capture live giant squid babies, or larvae. Giant squid larvae were successfully netted in waters off New Zealand and stored on the research ship, but died before reaching port. One day, marine biologists hope to raise giant squid from larvae in captivity.

Giant tube worms

To: Uncle Akira
From: Hanako
Subject: Giant tube worms
Attachment: Deepsea.doc

Dear Uncle Akira

I'm doing a project on marine animals, and I want to write about giant tube worms that live among hydrothermal vents. Because you're a marine biologist, I was hoping you'd be able to give me some information. I have attached some of my project research for you to look at.

Love

Hanako

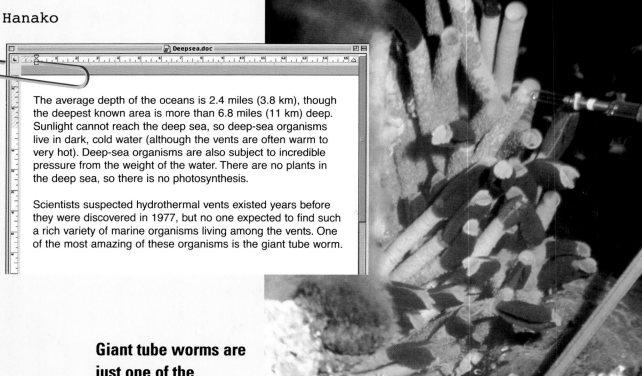

Deepsea.doc

The average depth of the oceans is 2.4 miles (3.8 km), though the deepest known area is more than 6.8 miles (11 km) deep. Sunlight cannot reach the deep sea, so deep-sea organisms live in dark, cold water (although the vents are often warm to very hot). Deep-sea organisms are also subject to incredible pressure from the weight of the water. There are no plants in the deep sea, so there is no photosynthesis.

Scientists suspected hydrothermal vents existed years before they were discovered in 1977, but no one expected to find such a rich variety of marine organisms living among the vents. One of the most amazing of these organisms is the giant tube worm.

Giant tube worms are just one of the organisms that live in total darkness among hydrothermal vents.

To: Hanako
From: Uncle Akira
Subject: Giant tube worms

Dear Hanako

Thanks for your email. Giant tube worms (Riftia pachyptila) are amazing animals. They live on the deep-sea floor around hydrothermal vents in tubes that they make. We know that:

Giant tube worms have four body parts:
- a red, head-like plume that can withdraw into the worm's tube when disturbed
- a collar, or bulge, inside the opening of the worm's tube
- a trunk or main body section
- a bottom part that anchors the worm to the tube

Giant tube worms have no mouth, no gut, and no anus. This means they do not have a digestive system! Yet they can grow almost 6.6 feet (2 m) long, so they must get energy from somewhere.

Giant tube worms stink, just like rotten eggs! Hydrogen sulfide stinks like rotten eggs, and bacteria at hydrothermal vents feed on hydrogen sulfide.

When biologists did more research, they discovered that the worms were full of bacteria. The plume of a giant tube worm acts like a gill. It lets substances in and out of the worm's body. A worm takes in hydrogen sulfide in seawater through its plume. The bacteria inside the worm feed on the hydrogen sulfide. In turn, the bacteria make food within the worm, which supplies the worm with energy.

Scientists also discovered that baby giant tube worms do have a mouth and a simple gut. That's how the worms take in bacteria. As the worms grow, the mouth disappears, the gut shuts, and the gut cells fill with bacteria.

Good luck with the rest of your project.

Love

Uncle Akira

Training to be a marine biologist

Marine biologists work in a number of different fields, but they all need to learn certain common skills. Marine biologists become qualified by studying at college.

At school

Marine biology is a science, so high school students who want to become marine biologists need to study subjects such as biology, math, chemistry, and English.

As part of their college studies, marine biology students gain practical experience.

Subjects marine biologists use are:

- biology to gain an understanding of all forms of life
- math to analyze data and solve problems, usually done on a computer
- chemistry to understand how chemicals in marine environments affect marine organisms
- English to communicate with other scientists, the media, and the public

Fact Box

A bachelor's degree takes four years to complete.

A college degree

After completing high school, people who want to study marine biology complete a Bachelor of Science or Bachelor of Arts degree at college. Students usually have a main area of study in biology or marine biology.

Farther study

Marine biology students who have completed their bachelor's degree can do more study, called graduate study. Graduate students take advanced courses in marine biology, and do research in specific areas of marine biology. Graduate studies can take many years to complete.

After their final year of college, most students begin working as professional marine biologists.

At work

Most marine biology students try to gain work experience in their field while they are studying at college. Once their college studies are finished, graduates often take jobs with government organizations, museums, aquariums, or colleges. Some graduates work in private industries, such as fisheries and marine-based tourism, while others work for businesses that give advice and suggestions on environmental issues.

On-the-job training

It is part of a marine biologist's job to attend seminars and conferences, read scientific papers and books, and learn about new scientific equipment. Marine biologists need to keep up to date with what is happening in their field.

Marine biologists are always learning!

Some marine biologists work with the public.

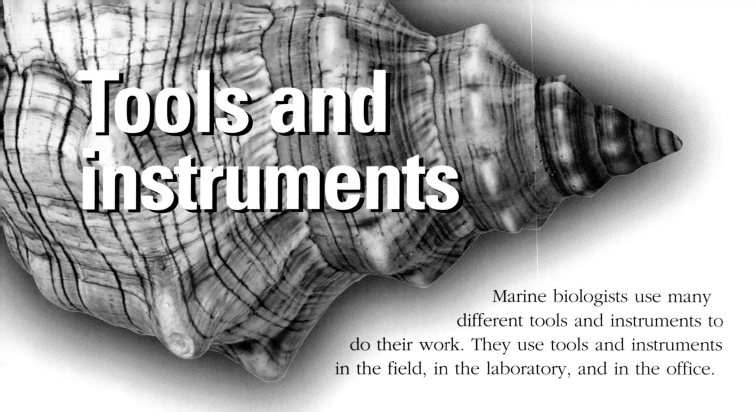

Tools and instruments

Marine biologists use many different tools and instruments to do their work. They use tools and instruments in the field, in the laboratory, and in the office.

Research vessel

Research vessels

A typical marine research vessel is a ship containing laboratories, scientific equipment, computers, tanks and freezers for samples, and a darkroom for developing film. There are also living quarters for the crew and scientists. A research vessel may also carry one or more submersibles.

Samplers

Marine samples are collected in a variety of ways. Special bottles are often used to collect water samples. Fine-mesh nets are often used to collect small organisms. Large-mesh nets, traps, dredges, grab samplers, or hooks are often used to catch larger organisms.

Submersible

Submersibles

A submersible is a small underwater vessel that is launched from a ship. It may or may not contain people. It collects data and samples using equipment such as video cameras, mechanical arms, and samplers. Submersibles can take scientists into the deep sea, where it is not possible for humans to scuba dive.

Scuba-diving equipment

Scuba-diving equipment

"Scuba" stands for **s**elf-**c**ontained **u**nderwater **b**reathing **a**pparatus. Basic scuba-diving equipment includes a protective wet or dry suit, a mask, fins, and a mouthpiece that connects to an air tank worn on the scuba diver's back. Scuba diving is one way of observing and studying marine life in its natural habitat.

Underwater camera

Underwater cameras

Underwater cameras are used to take photographs of marine organisms and their environments. Some cameras are set up to operate automatically, others are carried by scuba divers or on submersibles. Sometimes scientists even attach video cameras to large marine animals to record the animals' natural behavior.

Electronic tags

Electronic tags

Marine animals can be fitted with electronic tags that send and often record information about an animal's movements and other data. There are different types of tags. Some send information to machines set up on the sea floor or on a ship. Others send information to a satellite. The satellite then sends the information to computers on Earth. Some tags must be recovered before their data can be collected.

Sound recorders

Sound recorders

Oceans are noisy places. Marine biologists use sound recorders to record sounds made by marine animals. Marine biologists analyze the sounds. Marine animals can also be tracked by the sounds they make.

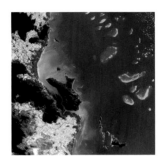

Remote-sensing image

Remote sensing

It is now possible to collect information about marine life and the oceans from a very long distance away. This is called remote sensing. Remote-sensing equipment includes powerful cameras and scanners. The equipment is usually carried aboard airplanes and satellites.

Photographs and images taken by remote sensing can supply marine biologists with information such as the amount of **chlorophyll** in an area, or the amount of vegetation along a coastline.

Microscope

Microscopes

Marine biologists look at samples through powerful microscopes. A microscope magnifies an object or a piece of an object so that it is easier to see.

Computer

Computers

Computers are used to store and analyze data. Marine biologists also use computers to write up reports and articles, to look up information on the Internet, and to send e-mails.

Pacific pelagics

February 5, 2002

TAGGING THE PACIFIC'S ANIMALS

Scientists from the U.S., Canada, Mexico, Japan, and the U.K. are working together to study the migration patterns of large open-ocean animals in the north Pacific Ocean.

The Tagging of Pacific **Pelagics** (TOPP) project is part of the 10-year Census of Marine Life. TOPP scientists aim to learn where open-ocean predators go over time and what factors control their migrations.

TOPP scientists will use electronic tags to track marine animals for periods ranging from months to years. Once the tags are attached to the animals, they collect data about the animals' behavior and location. The information can be stored on the tag or transmitted to satellites, then sent back to Earth where it can be analyzed and made available to scientists and the public.

During TOPP, thousands of animals from more than 20 different species will be tagged and tracked as they travel through the north Pacific Ocean. This will be the first time that a project follows several different species at once.

TOPP is expected to run for about 10 years and cost up to $30 million.

For further information go to http://www.toppcensus.org

Marine biologists attaching an electronic tag to an Atlantic bluefin tuna.

TRACKING SHARKS

In August, marine biologist Dr. Barbara Block and graduate students from Stanford University's Hopkins Marine Station captured and tagged salmon sharks in the Gulf of Alaska. The project, part of TOPP, began in September last year, and aims to test a new type of satellite tag.

Each shark had a satellite tag fitted to its **dorsal fin**. The tags do not transmit when they are under water, but when a shark surfaces, the tag's antenna is above the water. The tags contain radio transmitters that send the data to satellites. The information is then sent back to Earth, where Dr. Block and the students use it to plot the sharks' positions.

TOPP is interested in salmon sharks because they are predators that live in near-freezing waters. They maintain their body temperature above the water temperature. By tracking salmon sharks, scientists hope to discover where the sharks go and to learn more about the relationship between the sharks and their main food source, salmon.

Every tagged shark is currently sending back data. Dr. Block is anxious to learn how long the tags will last. Some tags have been transmitting continuously for almost a year.

Fact Box

Salmon sharks belong to the same family as white sharks and mako sharks.

An electronic tag is fitted to a salmon shark's dorsal fin.

Modern methods

Marine biologists work in the field, laboratories, and offices. They use the latest technology to help them study marine life.

In the field

Field work involves collecting data and samples from specific marine environments. It is relatively easy to collect data from coastal areas or shallow water, but the deep sea is a different matter. Humans cannot scuba dive in the deep sea. If scientists want to collect data from the deep sea, they use submersibles.

Alvin is a submersible owned by the United States Navy and operated by the Woods Hole Oceanographic Institution (WHOI). *Alvin* can hold a

pilot and two scientists, and can go down to a depth of 2.8 miles (4.5 km). *Alvin* takes about two hours to reach this depth. The deep sea is dark, so *Alvin* is fitted with powerful lights. During a dive, scientists inside *Alvin* have about four hours on the seabed to do experiments, take photographs, and collect samples. There are long waiting lists of scientists wanting to dive in submersibles like *Alvin*. Dives are carefully planned so that no time in the deep sea is wasted.

Some submersibles are operated remotely by a person on a research vessel.

***Alvin* is a submersible that has made more than 3,700 dives.**

In the laboratory

When marine biologists have the data and samples they need, they usually return to the laboratory to examine the samples and perform experiments. Marine biologists use a variety of equipment, including powerful microscopes, to examine samples.

Before a marine biologist can view a sample under a microscope, the sample must be prepared. The preparation and examination of the sample may go like this:

- Clean the sample.
- Slice the sample into sections.
- Add a dye or dyes to the sections.
- Place the sections on glass slides.
- Put a slide under a microscope.
- Examine the section.
- Photograph the section.
- Make notes about the section.

Marine biologists sometimes catch and observe live samples.

Sometimes live samples are collected. Marine biologists often put the organisms in glass tanks where they can be observed. Marine biologists must take great care to keep the samples alive. This means getting the water temperature, filters, lighting, and food just right. They must keep the tanks clean. Everything is done to keep the marine organisms as comfortable and calm as possible. Marine biologists will try to return live samples to the sea once their experiments are over.

In the office

Marine biologists analyze and write up the results of their experiments on a computer in their office. They also spend some time reading scientific papers, preparing talks for conferences, answering queries, and talking with other scientists.

Working on location

Marine biologists can face many challenges when studying marine organisms in their natural habitats. Marine organisms are found in all regions of the world, including polar, cold, subtropical and tropical regions, and at different ocean depths.

Antarctic algae

Antarctica is the coldest and windiest continent on Earth. There is no permanent human population in Antarctica. Visiting scientists stay at bases called research stations, or on board research vessels. Most scientists visit during the Antarctic summer and stay for only a few weeks or months.

Algae are one of the types of organisms that marine biologists study in Antarctica. Algae are plant-like organisms that live on water and land. They range in size from microscopic organisms to huge seaweeds. Algae make their own food by photosynthesis. The smallest algae are the single-celled marine algae that make up **phytoplankton**. Phytoplankton floats in the water and forms the base of the Antarctic food supply.

Marine biologists travel in research vessels to different areas around Antarctica to collect phytoplankton. Samples of phytoplankton and small marine animals that feed on phytoplankton are collected in nets, dredges, and grabs. Marine biologists can start to look at the samples in the laboratories on board the ship.

Fact Box

Marine biologists face many difficulties when they work in Antarctica. They are separated from their family and friends for long periods. They work in freezing, wet, and windy weather conditions, with only the equipment they brought with them. After all, in Antarctica you cannot just pop out to the store or office to pick up supplies.

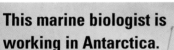

This marine biologist is working in Antarctica.

Coral reefs under attack

Coral reefs are beautiful places, full of a rich variety of marine organisms. Coral is an animal, and reefs form when living coral grows on top of coral skeletons.

The Great Barrier Reef is a chain of coral reefs off the coast of Queensland, Australia. But the coral is under attack. It is being eaten by crown-of-thorns sea stars, and the number of sea stars is growing. Marine biologists want to know why.

Coral reefs form in warm, shallow water, so marine biologists are able to observe coral and the sea stars. Marine biologists can observe from boats, surfboards, or by scuba diving. This makes it easy to collect samples and take photographs of the sea stars.

When crown-of-thorns sea star numbers suddenly increase, it is called an outbreak. During an outbreak, the sea stars eat coral faster than the coral can regrow. This threatens not only the reef, but the organisms that rely on the coral for food and shelter.

Marine biologists are studying whether outbreaks are natural or caused by human activities, such as:

- polluting the water with **nutrients**, so that more phytoplankton grows, which feeds more baby sea stars
- removing too many of the fish and other predators that feed on the sea star

More research is needed before marine biologists can be sure of the answers.

These crown-of-thorns sea stars are eating the coral underneath them.

Interview

Marah Newman, marine biologist

Marah Newman is a marine biologist at Scripps Institution of Oceanography.

What does your job involve?

I am doing a PhD (research project) in marine biology. I spend much of my time reading papers and studying work that relates to the **ecology** of coral reefs and how fishing impacts on these systems. I also study the organisms to learn about their distribution, eating habits, and ecological role on the reefs. A few wonderful weeks a year I get to go into the field and dive on the reefs, conducting surveys and studying the systems directly.

When did you first become interested in marine biology?

I spent my summers growing up in Cape Cod, and always loved the tide pools that formed at low tide. I spent hours watching the critters running around in their little worlds. When I was older (about 10 or 11) I became fascinated with sharks, and I spent time at Seacamp in the Florida Keys, where I learned to dive.

Where did you study?

I went to undergrad at Harvard. I spent a semester abroad at James Cook University in Townsville, Australia, and also studied there for a semester after I graduated from Harvard. I am now in my third year of the PhD program at Scripps.

22

Did you have a hero in your field?

Jacques Cousteau is always an inspiration, especially for his ability to communicate his passion to the public. Rachel Carson has also been an inspiration. She is not a marine biologist specifically, but her ability to write about nature and critically assess human beings' impact on the environment is truly magical.

What was your first job?

My first job in marine biology was as a volunteer and then staff member at the Bimini Biological Research Station in the Bahamas. Most of the work was tracking lemon sharks to study their daily movement patterns and homing abilities.

What do you think are the most important issues facing experts such as yourself?

I think marine biologists must make the effort to get the word out to the public and the government that we need drastic changes in the way we view and manage the oceans' resources, from fishing to development to oil exploration.

What would you like to achieve in your job in the future?

A lemon shark with other fish

I would like to help design protected areas and better fisheries management so that we can have fisheries that provide for people's needs without destroying the ecosystems of the sea. I would also like to contribute to public awareness of the threats that now face the world's oceans.

What advice would you give to young people interested in a career in marine biology?

Get out into nature as soon as you can. The more time you spend observing, the more you will learn about the systems that excite you and you will have your own questions about why and how certain things work. School is important because there are many ways of studying marine life: from molecular biology to modelling (using lots of math) to tracking animals (using statistics!). Most importantly, stay curious. Keep your eyes open wide so you can learn all that the sea has to teach us.

The case of the missing crab

Want to be a detective? Here's a case for you to solve. At the City Marine Laboratory, a crab named Christopher went missing last night. Well, most of him did. His empty shell was left in his tank.

What could have happened to Christopher? Read the detective's notes to find out!

Laboratory number 8

I began my investigation by going to laboratory number 8 where Christopher the crab lived. Many other marine animals are kept in tanks in the laboratory. There are some sea stars, various fish, another crab, and a giant Pacific octopus named Ollie. Each tank has a glass lid. There is a tiny gap between the lid and the pipe that feeds salt water into the tank.

I watched the animals being fed. Food is dropped into the tanks containing the sea stars, fish, and crab, but a jar with a screw-top lid is dropped into the octopus's tank. Inside the jar is the octopus's food: crab.

Ollie grabbed the jar with his arms. Then he unscrewed the lid! Ollie stuck an arm inside the jar and pulled out the crab. This is amazing! I need to do some research on octopuses.

Octopus research

A giant Pacific octopus:

- has eight arms covered with suckers
- does not have a skeleton and can squeeze into tiny places
- can change the color of its skin to match its surroundings
- can be 9.8 to 16.4 feet (3-5 m) long—it's the largest octopus
- gets its oxygen from seawater
- can swim, but often crawls along the seabed
- can shoot out a jet of ink when alarmed to confuse its attacker and to help the octopus escape
- can survive for a short time out of water
- is intelligent and gets bored easily, so in captivity it is often given puzzles to solve, like opening the lid on a jar

- belongs to the group of animals called mollusks
- likes to eat crabs, lobsters, shrimps, and fish
- mainly hunts at night

Solving the case

I think I know what happened to Christopher the crab last night, but, to be sure, I've decided to stay overnight in the laboratory.

11 P.M.

Ollie has just squeezed his body through the tiny gap in the lid of his tank! He started crawling towards the tank containing the remaining crab, but I stopped him just in time. Ollie ate Christopher last night, but Ollie's wandering days are over. I've returned him to his tank and made sure he can no longer escape.

Marine biology in the future

Humans value the oceans for many reasons. The oceans contain a great wealth of marine life. They provide us with food and materials. They are places of great beauty and mystery where people go to relax and play. They have an important role in the health and climate of our planet.

The work of marine biologists in the future will help us to understand, use, and protect the oceans. Their work will focus on several areas, including fisheries and **aquaculture**.

Huge quantities of seafood are taken from the sea each year in nets.

Fact Box

Scientists are using chemicals from marine organisms such as corals, algae, and sponges to develop drugs and products such as sunscreens. This growing industry is called marine biotechnology.

Fisheries

Fisheries operations harvest marine animals in order to sell them. A fishery is also the area where harvesting takes place.

Some fishery operations are small, but most are large corporations using ships fitted with the latest technology. These ships find and harvest huge quantities of marine animals.

If humans take too much seafood from the sea too quickly, stocks do not have a chance to recover. This affects the populations of the harvested animals, but it also affects other marine life. Organisms that rely on the harvested animals for food may starve, or the animals that are usually preyed upon by the harvested animals may increase in number.

Marine biologists can help fishery operations to harvest fish in the future. They can do this by studying marine populations, developing conservation plans, and shaping harvesting laws.

Aquaculture

Aquaculture is the farming of marine and freshwater organisms. The most commonly farmed animals are fish. They are kept in ponds, pools, coastal enclosures, or cages in water. Not only does aquaculture save wild fish stocks, but it also allows farmers to control what their fish are eating.

Most of the fish is sold as food, but some is used to restock lakes and rivers for recreational fishing, or as pets in home aquariums. Other water organisms are also farmed, such as oysters, scallops, mussels, lobsters, and seaweeds.

Aquaculture has problems. Setting up and running a farm costs a lot of money. With so many animals living so closely together, there is the risk of disease. Pollution from the animals' waste products is also a problem. Predators, such as seabirds, must be kept away, and the farmed animals must be kept from eating each other. Sometimes the natural environment is destroyed to build the farms.

Many people think these problems will be overcome and aquaculture will become an important way of conserving native marine life. By doing research into these problems, marine biologists will help to develop aquaculture in the future.

Marine and freshwater organisms are bred on aquaculture farms.

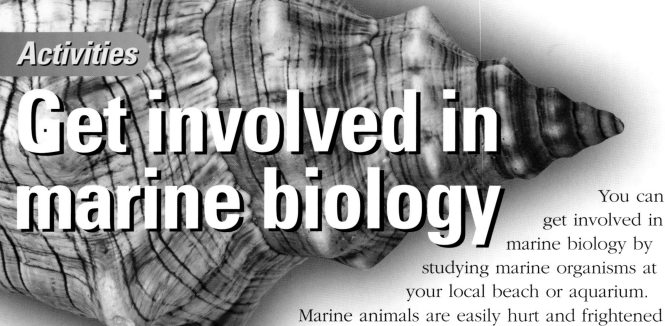

Get involved in marine biology

You can get involved in marine biology by studying marine organisms at your local beach or aquarium. Marine animals are easily hurt and frightened (and some bite or sting!), so it is best not to touch them. Here are some fun activities that you might like to try.

Make a tide pool chart

You will need:
- large sketchpad
- colored pencils
- magnifying glass
- encyclopedia, reference book, or Web site on marine life

What to do:

1 Find a tide pool at your local beach or aquarium.

2 Draw the outline of the tide pool in your sketchpad with a dark-colored pencil. You will be drawing marine organisms in your tide pool, so make sure your drawing is large enough.

3 Sketch the marine organisms in the tide pool. Use the right colors for each organism. Use a magnifying glass to look at the smaller animals.

4 Carefully label each organism. If you are not sure of a name or how to spell a word, look it up in an encyclopedia or marine biology reference book. You could also check out some marine biology Web sites.

5 Stick or tack your tide pool chart up on your wall. If you like, you could have it laminated first.

Solve a fishy puzzle

Do you know the name of this fish? It's a puzzle. Can you work it out?

You will need:
- piece of paper
- pencil
- encyclopedia, reference book, or Web site on marine life

What to do:
1 Look at the photograph of the fish on this page.
2 Read the questions on the right.
3 Write the answers on a piece of paper. If you do not know an answer, look the animal up in an encyclopedia or marine biology reference book. You could also check out some marine biology Web sites.
4 Put the first letters of the answers together to work out the fish's name.

Questions

Is coral a plant or an animal?

Do sharks and rays have skeletons made of bone? (Write yes or no.)

What do fish use to breathe?

How many arms does an octopus have?

What's the seven-letter name of an edible crustacean?

What are the flap-like parts of a fish's body that help it to move?

Animals with backbones are called vertebrates. What are animals without backbones called?

What's the largest fish in the world? The whale _ _ _ _ _.

What fish is also known as the slime eel?

(See page 32 for the answers.)

More to do

Get your whole class involved in marine biology!

- Put up charts of marine animals around your classroom.

- Ask your teacher to arrange a class trip to an aquarium or beach.

- Study a new marine animal each week.

- Ask a marine biologist to give a talk to your class.

Check it out!

A visit to an aquarium is a great way to learn about marine life.

Marine biology is an exciting science. You can learn more about marine biology, and the jobs of marine biologists, by checking out some of these places and Web sites.

The beach

You can begin studying marine biology simply by observing marine life at the beach. Always keep a notepad and pen handy to write down any interesting facts, or to make sketches. If you have a camera, start your own marine biology photo album. Some clubs and associations offer day trips to local beaches to examine marine life.

Aquariums or marine centers

An aquarium or marine center is a great place to learn about marine biology. At some marine centers, you can tour laboratories, examine marine samples, and go on boat trips. Many aquariums and marine centers have touch tanks where you can safely touch live marine organisms.

Web sites

Woods Hole Oceanographic Institution   **http://www.whoi.edu**

Scripps Institution of Oceanography   **http://www.sio.ucsd.edu**

Sea Grant marinecareers.net   **http://www.marinecareers.net**

Oceans Alive!   **http://www.mos.org/oceans**

Glossary

algae   plant-like organisms found on land and in water. Algae do not have true stems, leaves, or roots.

aquaculture   farming of marine and freshwater organisms

bacteria   microscopic organisms that have only one cell

chlorophyll   the green coloring in plants and plant-like organisms that traps sunlight during photosynthesis

conservation   protection of an environment, including organisms that live in that environment

crustaceans   a group of mostly marine animals with hard outer shells, such as crabs and lobsters

currents   large amounts of water that are pushed and moved by the wind in one direction

dorsal fin   a large fin on the back of a fish

ecology   the study of living things in their environments

ecosystems   communities of different organisms and the environments in which they live

fisheries   places where marine animals are harvested in order to sell them

habitat   the area in which an organism lives, feeds, and breeds

invertebrate   a type of animal that does not have a backbone

microscopic   too small to be seen with the naked eye, but able to be seen under a microscope

mollusks   a group of invertebrates that often have a shell, such as snails and oysters. Squids and octopuses are also mollusks

naturalist   a person who studies objects in nature

navigation   the process of directing the course of a vessel such as a ship

Norse mythology   traditional stories of fiction from Norway, usually about imaginary people or creatures

nutrients   substances that help organisms to live, grow, and stay healthy

pelagics   animals living in the open ocean

photosynthesis   the process in which plants and plant-like organisms make food from sunlight, water, and the gas carbon dioxide

phytoplankton   plant-like organisms that are part of plankton

salinity   the amount of salt in water

sonar   **so**und **na**vigation **a**nd **r**anging, a method of finding objects in water using sound echoes

submersibles   small underwater vessels that are launched from a ship

Index

Page 29 Fishy Puzzle answers:

animal, no, gills, eight, lobster, fins, invertebrates, shark, hagfish

Name of fish: angelfish